ESSENTIAL

IRA AND 401(K)
INVESTING

DALLAS SALISBURY
AND
MARC ROBINSON

DORLING KINDERSLEY

London • New York • Sydney • Delhi • Paris • Munich • Johannesburg

London, New York, Munich, Melbourne, Delhi

Editors Ruth Strother, Stephanie Rubenstein
Consultant Mark Johnson
Design and Layout Hedayat Sandjari
Photography Anthony Nex
Project Editor Crystal A. Coble
Project Art Editor Mandy Earey
DTP Designer Jill Bunyan
Photo Research Mark Dennis, Sam Ruston
Indexing Rachel Rice
Editorial Director LaVonne Carlson
Design Director Tina Vaughan
Publisher Sean Moore

First American Edition, 2000
05 10 9 8 7 6 5 4 3

Published in the United States by
DK Publishing, Inc.
375 Hudson Street,
New York, New York 10014
**See our complete product line at
www.dk.com**

Packaged by Top Down Productions
Copyright © 2000
DK Publishing, Inc.
Text copyright © 2000 Marc Robinson

DK Publishing, Inc. offers special discounts for bulk purchases for sales promotions or premiums. Specific, large quantity needs can be met with special editions, including personalized covers, excerpts of existing guides, and corporate imprints. For more information, contact Special Markets Dept., D K Publishing, Inc., 375 Hudson Street, NY, NY 10014; Fax: (800) 600-9098

A CIP catalog record for this book is available from the Library of Congress

ISBN 0-7894-7171-x

Reproduced by Colourscan, Singapore
Printed in China

The information contained in this publication is general in nature and is not intended to provide advice, guidance, or expertise of any nature regarding financial or investment decisions. Neither DK Publishing Inc., Marc Robinson, Top Down, or Ronald W. Johnson make any representations or warranties with respect to the professional experience or credentials of the authors or contributors, or to the merits of the information of materials contained herein. The reader should consult independent financial advisors and investment professionals prior to making any decision or plan.

CONTENTS

401(K)S

OTHER TYPES OF PLANS

INVESTMENT STRATEGIES

INTRODUCTION

S aving money for retirement can be frustrating if you don't know what to invest in or where to start. Depending upon your situation, you may have many options. Each one may have different requirements, be designed for specific investors, and have different tax consequences. IRA and 401(k) Investing will guide you through the process of deciding which plan or plans may be best suited for you. It will tell you what each plan is, how it works, and how to evaluate it. If you haven't already begun investing, reading this book will prepare you to start investing your money to secure your future. Understanding all your options is the first step toward a financially secure retirement.

SAVING FOR YOUR FUTURE

It's never too early or too late to save for retirement.
Every day and every little bit of money helps add
to the security of your future.

SEEKING SHELTER

There are a number of retirement plans that qualify for tax breaks. Any of them has the power to boost your long-term savings more effectively than a regular savings program.

TIME IS MONEY

It's easy to rationalize not saving money. You can say that putting away small amounts isn't going to help much in retirement. Here's one reason why you're wrong.

Small amounts add up. Consider the following example—or calculate it with any amount you choose. If you want to have $100,000 in 30 years and invest safely for a mere 5% after-tax rate of return, you will need to put away $120 a month. If you try to save $100,000 in only 10 years, you will need to put away $641 a month.

THE TAX CAT ▼
Tax-qualified retirement plans allow you to reinvest earnings instead of paying annual taxes. That means all of your money continues to grow without any being grabbed by the IRS.

▲ TAX SHELTER

Although most financial professionals like to use the phrase tax-advantaged accounts *instead of* tax sheltered accounts, *most people more easily understand the latter: a type of account that shelters your money (the bird in hand) from taxation. IRAs, 401(k)s, and other* tax-qualified *retirement accounts fall into this category.*

SURVEY SHOWS SOME ARE UNPREPARED

The 1999 Retirement Confidence Survey, conducted by the Employee Benefit Research Institute (EBRI), found that 6% of people age 54 or older had saved nothing for retirement, and 11% of the people in that age group had saved under $10,000.

THE POWER OF DEFERRING TAXES

Tax-sheltered retirement accounts are specifically designed to save you taxes and entice you to save. Here's an explanation of why retirement plans pay off.

Shelter your money. Retirement accounts are not investments themselves; they're the "housing" for your investments. For example, when you buy a stock in a regular personal account, the dividends it pays are taxable. But if you buy that same stock and put it in your retirement account, those same dividends aren't taxed—until that money is taken out of the account. Only then does the IRS take its piece. Since all of your money continues to work for you, there's more money to earn more money. (Note: Roth IRAs are the exception. Earnings aren't taxed when withdrawn.)

For example. Suppose you contribute $1,800 a year to a tax-sheltered retirement account. If your money earns 8% a year, you will have $233,359 in 30 years. If, however, you put that $1,800 a year into a taxable account, and you're in the 28% bracket, you will only have $148,473 in 30 years.

What if you have 20 years—instead of 30—until retirement? The same $1,800 a year will give you $92,228 in 20 years, compared to $69,489 in a taxable account after 20 years.

IS SOCIAL SECURITY ENOUGH?

I f you're planning to live on your Social Security check someday, get ready for a drastic reduction in your lifestyle. Here are the main reasons why Social Security won't be enough.

IT WON'T REPLACE YOUR PRERETIREMENT WAGES

According to the American Association of Retired Persons (AARP), if you have average earnings throughout your career and retire at the full retirement age, Social Security benefits will replace 43% of the income you earn during the year before you retire.

In fact, some experts predict that Social Security benefits could run out altogether—somewhere around 2037.

RETIREMENT AGE IS RISING

Although the current age for full retirement is 65, this age will be gradually increased to 67. A greatly reduced Social Security benefit is available at age 62. Anyone who hopes to retire earlier than that can't count on Social Security at all.

A THREE-LEGGED STOOL ▶

When financial planners advise clients about planning for retirement, they often use a three-legged stool analogy. If Social Security is the only leg of the stool you have available, you won't be sitting pretty when it's time to retire. A secure retirement may depend upon taking full advantage of all three legs shown here.

Social Security

Personal Taxable Savings

Retirement Plans

THINGS TO KNOW

- Social Security offers an online retirement planner that permits you to make a fairly detailed projection of what your benefits are likely to be. Try it for yourself at this web address: www.ssa.gov/retire. You can also call the Social Security Administration at 800-772-1213 to receive a copy of your Personal Earnings and Benefit Estimate Statement.

- You may want to check your Social Security records on a regular basis to be sure that you've been credited with all of your earnings, since your benefit will depend upon the accuracy of the information.

When you reach full retirement age, you will get your benefits with no limit on your earnings.

IT WON'T PROTECT AGAINST INFLATION

Even if you can live on your Social Security check, it won't necessarily guard against inflation.

- Although most people live on less than their current income in retirement, inflation can gradually erode the purchasing power of their checks. For example, Social Security beneficiaries receive a cost-of-living adjustment based upon the Consumer Price Index, but the benefit may not keep pace with the rising costs of healthcare and other expenses.

- You might need long-term care at some point. Long-term care expenses can be $40,000 per year or more and, for now, are rising rapidly.

AN INVERSE ▶ RELATIONSHIP

According to AARP, if you earn the minimum wage throughout your career, your Social Security benefit will replace 59% of your preretirement salary; if you make the maximum wage on which Social Security is withheld ($76,200 in the tax year 2000), your benefit will replace roughly 24% of your preretirement wages; if you make more than $76,200 (in 2000), the amount your Social Security benefit will replace is dependent upon your pre-Social Security net income.

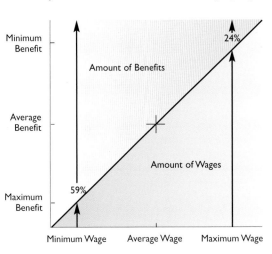

SAVINGS SUGGESTIONS

*M*any people look into their pockets and believe they don't have anything left to save. There are ways, however, to create a savings plan for yourself. Here are three suggestions.

PAY YOURSELF FIRST

Sign up for savings and investment plans that take the money out before you get your hands on it. If you never see it, you won't spend it. Pretty soon, you will forget it's missing and be comfortable living on less.

For example, when you get extra money such as gifts or bonuses, pay yourself first by putting at least part of it in a savings account or an investment vehicle. When your car loan is paid off, take the money you would have used to pay the debt and save it.

Dividend reinvestment plans are a good way to pay yourself first. You receive dividends from mutual funds you own. You can automatically have those dividends buy more shares instead of paying out the money to you. If you own stock, ask the company if it has a dividend reinvestment plan.

2 You may need to look no further than your own pockets to find enough money to make a difference.

TAKE A SELF-TEST

Keep track of every expenditure, large or small, for a week. You will see that you could easily forego some of those purchases. The small amounts you're wasting each day can help you save for retirement. Say, for example, you spend $2.50 on a cup of gourmet coffee every morning on the way to work at your local coffee emporium. That's $12.50 a week, or $650 per year—a significant amount of money each year that could be working for you towards your retirement.

THE EARLY BIRD

It pays for you to make your contributions as early in the year as possible, because your money will have more time to grow. You can arrange for the total annual amount you have allocated to be deducted in installments from a checking or savings account.

USE AUTOMATIC INVESTMENT PROGRAMS

Automatic investment plans are perfect for people who have trouble saving because the plans don't require discipline. You fill out the paperwork and the rest is automatic. Automatic investing also helps you take advantage of a basic investment strategy called Dollar-Cost Averaging (see pg 66-67).

An opportunity for automatic investing is offered through most mutual funds. Simply sign up (on the application) to have the fund deduct an amount from your checking account each month. Many funds permit you to invest even very small amounts if you agree to an ongoing investment program,

PAYROLL DEDUCTION

Participating in a company retirement plan is a powerful form of automatic savings, because a portion of your paycheck is automatically deducted every time and contributed to the plan. Even though you're saving money automatically, your take-home pay won't be that much less. The reason is that the money you're saving reduces the amount of tax you owe. You would have lost some of the money you're saving in taxes anyway. In addition to retirement plans, you can use payroll deduction to buy savings bonds and other investments.

---

3 Once you factor in taxes, deductions from your paycheck aren't really as much as they may seem.

EASIER THAN ▶ YOU THINK
You can add a lot of money to your retirement account with very little effort—other than the initial effort of believing you can live on less.

IRAs

IRAs are a great way to save taxes and put away money for your future. This chapter gives you an overview of the key points regarding the various IRAs available.

TRADITIONAL IRAs

A mutual fund company did a survey and found that one in three people don't know what "IRA" means. If you fall within that category, here's the short course.

WHAT'S AN IRA?

IRA stands for Individual Retirement Account. The main advantage of traditional IRAs is they generally offer an immediate tax deduction, along with tax-deferred growth of the money in the account. Even though traditional IRAs can reduce your current tax obligation, other IRAs may provide other tax breaks that may be better suited for you.

HOW AN IRA WORKS ▶
This pictogram explains how a traditional IRA works. The birdcage with the money bird inside represents a shelter for your money, while the cat represents the IRS. You will see this symbolism used throughout the book.

YOU CONTRIBUTE EARNINGS

You can contribute some of your annual earnings and may be able to deduct some or all of it from your taxable income for the year.

Contribution limits. The maximum you can contribute to an IRA is $2,000.

Contribution deadline. An IRA contribution is only tax deductible if it's made by the tax filing deadline for the previous year. For example, your contribution for the 2001 tax year must be made by April 15, 2002. Even if you file for an extension, the contribution must be made by April 15.

SAVINGS GROW TAX-DEFERRED

All of the money earned in your IRA goes untaxed until you withdraw it so you have more money working for you. This can lead to a significant increase in overall earnings through the years. The more years you save in the IRA, the more significant the tax-deferral becomes.

The term tax-deferred comes from the fact that your income taxes are deferred (postponed) as long as the money remains invested.

MONEY IS TAXED AT WITHDRAWAL

Once you turn 70 1/2, you must begin withdrawing money. The money you withdraw may be taxable by federal, state, or local agencies.

You're permitted, however, to withdraw money without penalty once you turn 59 1/2. Before that age, withdrawals could be subject to tax penalties in addition to income taxes unless you follow one of several rules that allow you to withdraw money without penalty before you turn 59 1/2.

IT'S A FACT

ERISA (Employee Retirement Income Security Act) was first established in 1974. It governs IRAs and all other retirement plans.

CRITERIA FOR TRADITIONAL IRAs

B *e sure you're eligible to make a contribution to a traditional IRA. As is the case with most tax breaks, you have to meet certain eligibility requirements to qualify.*

WHO'S ELIGIBLE?

Not everyone is eligible to make tax-deductible contributions to a traditional IRA. Here are the major factors.

Age. You must be younger than 70 1/2 by the end of the year in which you make the contribution.

Taxable income. You must have received taxable income (including wages, salaries, bonuses, commissions, tips, etc.) during the year. Pension income, rental income, interest, dividends, and disability don't qualify.

Income limit. If your income is too high, you may not qualify for a tax deduction. If you're single, you can only take a full IRA deduction if your modified adjusted gross income is below $32,000 in the year 2000. That income limit will rise each year until 2005, when the cap will be $50,000.

Marital income limit. If you're married, you can still take a full IRA deduction on your 2000 tax return if your joint income is below $52,000. The income limit will jump each year until 2007 when the cap reaches $80,000.

Annual adjustments. Each year, the income limits on qualifying for a partial IRA deduction will rise. The tax deduction, however, gets smaller as you near the limit. In the year 2000, the partial IRA deduction phases out when your income hits $42,000. For a married couple filing jointly, the partial deduction phases out at $62,000.

WHAT IS INCOME?

Your modified adjusted gross income is not always the same as your adjusted gross income. When you add up your modified adjusted gross income to determine your eligibility for a traditional IRA, you must include certain income such as interest from tax-free bonds. Keep in mind: You're only using that income to see if you're eligible to make a traditional IRA contribution. It isn't included in your taxable income.

LIMITATION EXCEPTION

You may still qualify to make a deductible IRA contribution if you earn more than the maximum income limits. The catch is that neither you nor your spouse can be an active participant in an employer-sponsored retirement plan. An employer-sponsored retirement plan includes a pension, profit-sharing, 401(k), or some other program set up by the employer for the benefit of its employees.

4 The IRS doesn't permit you to take a loan from an IRA and repay with interest.

SPECIAL SPOUSAL RULES

A stay-at-home spouse qualifies more easily for a tax-deductible contribution to a traditional IRA. Generally, that spouse can claim a full tax deduction as long as the couple's adjusted gross income is less than $150,000. It doesn't matter whether or not the employed spouse participates in an employer-sponsored retirement plan.

RULES FOR CHILDREN

If you want your child to be a millionaire someday, a good way to start is by opening an IRA for him or her at as young an age as possible. There's no minimum age requirement to open an IRA. The only requirement is that the child must have earned compensation for the year. That can come by doing chores for neighbors or even selling lemonade. If you own your own business, you may even be able to find work for your kids and put them on the payroll.

◀ **TREASURE AHEAD**
Since there's no minimum age requirement on having an IRA, any child old enough to be paid for chores or odd jobs can open one. In addition, all of the child's earnings, up to $2,000 a year, can be contributed, making the reward at the end that much richer.

MOVING YOUR MONEY

Having your money locked up in an IRA doesn't mean it has to stay in the same place forever. There are two main ways to move your funds without triggering a tax consequence.

TRANSFER IT DIRECTLY

The bank, mutual fund, or brokerage firm that manages your IRA is called a *trustee* or *custodian*. If you follow the rules, you can transfer the IRA from one trustee or custodian to another without causing yourself a tax problem. These *direct transfers* are not subject to any taxes or penalties.

Although the IRS doesn't mind you transferring an IRA from one trustee to another, the trustee losing your account may try to discourage you. For example, there may be a fee to close your account or there may be some other penalty imposed. Always check the paperwork you received when the IRA was opened (or ask a customer service representative) to see what restrictions and qualifications may be involved.

Also be sure you know how long the transfer will take. It may take longer than you think.

5 The IRS doesn't place any limits on the number of times you can transfer an IRA each year.

60-DAY LOANS

Sometimes, people take a distribution and hope to use their funds for 60 days. There are no taxes or penalties as long as all the money is replaced and rolled over within 60 days. The danger is in failing to replace the money and rolling it over within 60 days. You will have to pay income taxes on the money plus a 10% early withdrawal penalty. Remember, IRAs aren't meant to be short-term loans.

ROLLOVERS OF AFTER-TAX CONTRIBUTIONS

If you leave an employer and want to move your 401(k) savings, you won't be allowed to roll over the portion of your account that constitutes your after-tax contributions into an IRA. You can roll over, however, the earnings from those contributions. Even though you can't roll over after-tax contributions, they won't be included in your income (because you've already paid taxes on that money) and therefore won't be subject to a 10% penalty for premature withdrawal.

ROLL IT OVER

You might decide to take a distribution or payout from your IRA instead of having the funds transferred directly to another IRA trustee or custodian. By putting the money in your hands, you risk paying taxes and IRS penalties for what's called a *premature withdrawal.*

To avoid taxes and penalties, the distribution or payout must be rolled over to another IRA in 60 days or less.

Unlike transfers, you are only permitted one rollover in a 12-month period.

When you leave a job. A Qualified Domestic Relations Order (QDRO) may be rolled over into a qualified retirement plan if the payee is a spouse or ex-spouse (but not a child) and if the distributions would qualify for a rollover if they were paid to the plan participant. For example, if a plan is making substantially equal payments over ten years or more, they're not eligible for a tax-free rollover.

WITHDRAWALS WITHOUT PENALTIES

A lthough withdrawals from IRAs are discouraged, there are ways to take out your money without a penalty.

▼ **SPECIFIC CIRCUMSTANCES**
If any one of these situations occurs, you or your beneficiaries will be able to make withdrawals from your IRA without incurring a penalty.

OR

THE CAGE OPENS

Even though they're called retirement accounts, IRAs can be tapped before you officially retire. Keep in mind, however, that an IRA may be your most powerful way to invest to earn the most for your later years. You may, therefore, decide you're better off tapping other sources of cash if possible.

IT'S A FACT

According to a recent study, more than 25% of Americans believe the lottery is their best opportunity to fund their retirement.

AGE

Although much has changed about IRAs in recent years, the magic date is still age 59 1/2. When you reach that milestone, you can take as much or as little money as you want from your IRA without being subject to a 10% premature withdrawal penalty.

If you're taking money from a traditional IRA, these withdrawals will be taxed at your income tax rate that applies that year. All withdrawals are considered ordinary income, not capital gains.

DISABILITY

Suppose you aren't age 59 1/2 but must take money out of your IRA because you can't earn a living. The rules governing IRAs permit people to withdraw funds under these circumstances without a 10% penalty.

What qualifies. You must suffer from a genuine disability, not a temporary inconvenience. This is defined as a disability of long, continuous, and indefinite duration. You must be able to show proof that you can't perform any substantial employment activity.

DEATH

The IRS lets your beneficiary or your estate avoid a penalty if you die. On the other hand, payments from an IRA may cause estate tax problems (see pg. 32 for more details).

OR

MEDICAL EXPENSES

The 10% premature withdrawal penalty won't be applied if you withdraw money to pay for certain medical expenses. You can't, for example, make a penalty-free withdrawal for every doctor visit. But you can withdraw money to pay for medical expenses that aren't covered by insurance. Most of all, the expenses must exceed 7.5% of your adjusted gross income—so they will have to be major expenditures.

Here's an example of how that works. If your income is $30,000 per year, your medical expenses must exceed $2,250 (7.5% of $30,000) before you may start withdrawing from your IRA without penalty.

▼ **NO PENALTY, BUT STILL A TAX**

While you avoid the premature tax penalty under the circumstances shown here, you will still be responsible for paying any income that may be due based on the money you withdraw.

19

MORE WAYS TO WITHDRAW

F ortunately, an IRA can be tapped before age 59 1/2 without your having to prove that something terrible has happened to you. The IRA rules now permit penalty-free withdrawals in the following situations.

AN ALTERNATIVE

To avoid depleting retirement assets to pay for a child's tuition, books, and other expenses, consider starting an Education IRA for your children (see pg 30-31 for more details).

HEALTH INSURANCE

You can avoid the premature withdrawal penalty if you meet each and every one of the following conditions:

- You lost your job;
- You received unemployment compensation for 12 or more consecutive weeks;
- The money is withdrawn during the year you received unemployment benefits or during the following year;
- The withdrawals stop within 60 days after you're employed again.

Taxes due. If you meet all of these conditions, you won't pay the 10% penalty, but you will still be responsible for paying income taxes at ordinary income tax rates on the total amount withdrawn.

COLLEGE EXPENSES

You won't pay the 10% penalty if you withdraw money to pay for qualified higher education expenses. It's not just your own educational expenses that permit you to avoid the penalty. The expenses can be related to college costs for your spouse, or for any child or grandchild of yourself or your spouse. The person doesn't have to be listed as a dependent on your income tax return.

6 "Making a withdrawal" and "receiving a distribution" mean the same thing.

FIRST-TIME HOMEBUYER COSTS

You can make a penalty-free withdrawal from an IRA if the money is used to buy, build, or rebuild a house that will be the principal residence for you, your spouse, child, grandchild, or ancestor of you or your spouse. The term *ancestor* includes a parent or grandparent.

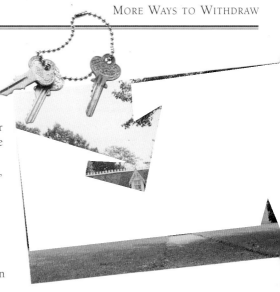

You can't take out more than $10,000 for this purpose, and the money must be used within 120 days.

The IRS is fairly lenient in how it defines *first-time homebuyer*. The major restriction is that neither you nor your spouse may have had an ownership interest in a principal residence during the two years prior to buying or building a new principal residence.

Hidden expense. Taking $10,000 out of your IRA to help pay for a child's downpayment on a house can cost you a lot more than $10,000 down the road. Remember you're also losing the earnings you would have made on that money if it was still in your IRA. Even though you won't pay a premature withdrawal penalty, you will pay taxes on the withdrawal. So, in the end, you will end up losing a lot more than $10,000.

7 The penalty exemption available to first-time home buyers who withdraw money from an IRA doesn't apply to money withdrawn from 401(k)s.

8 Non-deductible (after-tax) contributions to an IRA can be rolled over and are tax-free when taken as distributions, because you have already paid taxes on the contribution.

MANDATORY WITHDRAWALS

*S*ome people aren't in a hurry to take their IRA money. They'd like to leave all of it for a beneficiary. The IRS, however, wants to finally begin taxing the money, so they have rules that require you to start withdrawing money by a certain age.

AGE

If you have a traditional IRA, withdrawals must begin by age 70 1/2. You must make the first withdrawal in the year you turn 70 1/2 or you can wait until April 1 of the following year.

The problem with waiting until the following year is that you must take your second withdrawal by December 31 of that same year. As a consequence, you wind up with two withdrawals in the same year—and that could potentially throw you into a higher tax bracket.

CALCULATING THE CORRECT AMOUNT

The amount you must withdraw must be based upon your life expectancy, or the joint life expectancy of you and your beneficiary. Although the government wants you to begin withdrawing money, it doesn't want you or your beneficiary to outlive your money. Therefore, in cases where the calculation is based on a joint life expectancy and your beneficiary is younger than you, you will be allowed to take out less money without being penalized.

WARNING!

Failing to make the mandatory withdrawal can subject you to serious penalties. You could be hit with a 50% tax penalty on the amount that should have been withdrawn.

LEARNING ABOUT INCOME AVERAGING

Read about 10-year income averaging in the instructions for IRS Form 4972 (electing 10-year averaging and calculating the 10-year income averaging tax). See www.irs.ustreas.gov/prod/forms_pubs/forms.html

9 Form 4972 provides a checklist to determine income averaging eligibility.

WITHDRAWING SUBSTANTIALLY EQUAL AMOUNTS

If you're in a hurry to get at your money, you may begin withdrawals without penalty prior to turning 59 1/2. You may withdraw money in substantially equal amounts. The rules here apply to all IRA assets. They only apply to 401(k) assets, however, if you or your spouse no longer works for the employer of that 401(k). Be sure to consult a tax professional regarding your own situation.

Minimum number of times. You must make at least one withdrawal a year.

Minimum number of years. Withdrawals must continue for at least five years or until you reach 59 1/2, whichever is longer.

Control over investments. You can continue to make investment decisions about the assets still in the account.

Money can remain. The account doesn't have to be empty after your last withdrawal.

Three methods. There are three methods for determining the amount of periodic withdrawals (ask your tax advisor).

ROTH IRAS

R oth IRAs are a recent addition to the retirement savings landscape. A Roth IRA is basically the same as a traditional IRA, except for an important tax difference.

MONEY IS TAXED BEFORE IT GOES IN

You can't deduct contributions to a Roth IRA. Instead, you pay any income tax due on earnings that you contribute to your Roth IRA account. This is the opposite of traditional IRAs, where you contribute untaxed earnings and pay taxes on the money when it's withdrawn.

PAY THE ▶ TAX CAT FIRST
You can contribute after-tax dollars to a Roth IRA. The withdrawals from this type of account are usually tax-free because you've already paid taxes on your contribution.

NO CONTRIBUTION AGE LIMIT

Age is irrelevant. As long as you're earning money and pay any taxes due on that money, you can contribute to a Roth IRA.

CONTRIBUTION PERIOD IS EXTENDED

Your Roth IRA contribution must be made by the tax filing deadline for the previous year. As an example, the contribution for the 2001 tax year must be made by April 15, 2002. Even if you file for an extension, the contribution must be made by April 15.

SAVINGS MAY BE FREE FROM TAXES

The attraction of a Roth IRA is that all of your contributions and earnings are sheltered from taxes so they can grow without being depleted along the way.

10 Although you won't pay federal income taxes, make sure your state doesn't tax withdrawals from a Roth IRA.

NO WITHDRAWAL AGE LIMIT

With a Roth IRA, you don't have to take out the money by any particular age. You can leave it in the account to grow tax-free if you're doing well enough without it.

WITHDRAWALS ARE TYPICALLY TAX-FREE

The only requirements are that you leave the money in the account for at least five years and you're 59 1/2 when you withdraw the money.

TAXPAYER RELIEF

The Taxpayer Relief Act of 1997 changed retirement planning significantly. It created the Roth IRA, which offers enormous opportunities to save for retirement and eliminates many of the reasons why people avoided IRAs previously. Even though they do not offer an immediate tax deduction, Roth IRAs have incredible tax advantages. The Taxpayer Relief Act also created the education IRA, reduced the tax on capital gains, and gave a tax break to homeowners selling their primary dwelling for a large profit.

ROTH ELIGIBILITY

A lot more people qualify to contribute to a Roth IRA than are eligible for a traditional IRA. In fact, many people who are eligible for a traditional IRA choose to contribute to the Roth IRA instead. Here's how to tell if you qualify.

CONTRIBUTIONS

Contributions can be made to a Roth IRA, no matter how young you are. Before you set up a Roth IRA for that newborn, however, check out the taxable compensation requirement in the next column (Income).

Single. You can contribute up to $2,000 a year or 100% of earned income, whichever is less.

Married. You can each contribute up to $4,000 a year or 100% of earned income, whichever is less.

 If you're eligible, you may contribute to a Roth IRA even if you participate in an employer-sponsored plan.

INCOME

You must have received taxable compensation during the year. In most cases, you can contribute to a Roth IRA if you have taxable compensation (which includes wages, salaries, tips, bonuses, commissions, and other money). Even though your Social Security check is income and may be taxable, it doesn't satisfy the requirement to make a Roth IRA contribution.

Unless you make a very high income, you will probably qualify for a Roth IRA.

Single. If you're single, you can make a full contribution if your modified adjusted gross income is no more than $95,000. A partial contribution is permitted if your modified adjusted gross income is no more than $110,000.

Married. If you're married, you can still make a full contribution, as long as your modified adjusted gross income is no more than $150,000. If you're married, filing jointly, the limit for a partial contribution is $160,000.

Modified adjusted gross income. For some people, modified adjusted gross income is different from just plain adjusted gross income. You have to add in certain amounts, such as deductions for student loan interest, when determining if you qualify for the Roth IRA.

A Roth IRA or a Traditional IRA?

The main difference between a traditional IRA and a Roth IRA is the distinction between tax-deferred versus tax-free. *Tax-deferred* (IRAs) means that money will be subject to income taxes when withdrawn. *Tax-free* (Roth IRAs) means that money won't be taxed when withdrawn. Income contributed to an IRA, however, isn't taxed in the year it's earned. Income contributed to a Roth IRA is taxed in the year it's earned.

Avoiding Penalties

Here's how to make sure your tax-free withdrawals stay tax-free. You may also face a 10% penalty for early withdrawals unless you meet one of the following exceptions:

- You're 59 1/2;
- You're disabled;
- The distribution is made to a beneficiary or your estate after your death;
- You use the money to pay certain qualified first-time home buyer expenses;
- The distributions are part of a series of substantially equal payments;
- You have significant medical expenses that aren't reimbursed;
- You're paying health insurance premiums after a job loss;
- The distributions are not more than qualified higher education expenses;
- The distribution is prompted because of an IRS lien on the qualified plan.

Although you can avoid the penalty by meeting one of these exceptions, the distribution is not necessarily free from income taxation. You may also lose the feature that caused you to open up a Roth IRA in the first place—tax-free withdrawals. So be careful about withdrawing money before the Roth IRA rules permit it. Consult a tax advisor.

> **12** You're always able to withdraw your original contributions to a Roth IRA without paying a penalty or federal taxes.

Converting to a Roth IRA

B ecause Roth IRAs are relatively new, most people are the owners of traditional IRAs. Nevertheless, if the Roth IRA features appeal to you, you're permitted to convert a traditional IRA to a Roth IRA.

General Rules

If you want to convert your traditional IRA to a Roth IRA, there are two requirements that must be met:

- As a general rule, your modified adjusted gross income can't be more than $100,000;
- If you're married, you can't be filing a separate tax return.

Converting a traditional IRA to a Roth IRA has immediate tax consequences. When you convert all or part of a traditional IRA to a Roth IRA, it's almost as if you withdrew the money, but aren't charged a penalty. You're taxed on the amount converted.

You don't have to convert all your traditional IRAs to Roth IRAs at one time. You can stagger the conversions over a number of tax years or keep them as traditional IRAs.

13 A required minimum distribution from an IRA (for people who have reached age 70 1/2) may not be rolled over or converted into a Roth IRA.

Consult First

Many financial websites offer software that lets you determine if converting to a Roth IRA makes sense for you. It's a big decision with significant ramifications, so you should consult a tax advisor on your specific situation before making any conversion.

14 You can transfer a portion of a traditional IRA account to a Roth IRA. You don't have to transfer the entire amount.

 15 If you're in a high tax bracket during your working years and expect to be in a low tax bracket once you retire, the Roth IRA may not provide much advantage over a traditional IRA.

WHY CONVERT?

If you're going to get taxed anyway on the amount transferred to a Roth IRA, why do it? Assuming you're in the same tax bracket now as years from now, the difference is the amount you expect to make on your investment. Let's look at two examples:

● Suppose you have $50,000 in a traditional IRA and in 15 years it grows to $150,000. You will pay taxes on the entire $150,000 as it is withdrawn;

● In contrast, let's assume you convert the $50,000 in a traditional IRA to a Roth IRA. You will pay taxes on the $50,000 when you make the conversion. If the $50,000 (assume no taxes just for this example) grows to $150,000 in 15 years, you will owe no taxes as the money is withdrawn. Essentially, the $100,000 you made on your money in the Roth IRA is tax-free. The only difference is that you will probably pay the tax on the $50,000 a lot sooner than you would, if you didn't convert to a Roth IRA.

IT'S A FACT

The Roth IRA was named for Senator Roth of Delaware, its key proponent.

ROLLOVER TREATMENT

The conversion from a traditional IRA to a Roth IRA is treated as a rollover. The conversion is handled in one of the following ways:

● The funds from the traditional IRA come to you and you must contribute it to the Roth IRA within 60 days;

● The trustee of the traditional IRA transfers the amount to be converted directly to the trustee of the Roth IRA;

● The trustee of the traditional IRA simply redesignates it as a Roth IRA, assuming you're keeping the money in the same place.

EDUCATION IRAS

*I*n reality, the education IRA is not a retirement account, but a savings vehicle to help pay for a child's or grandchild's education. Although the contribution to an education IRA isn't deductible, the amount contributed and its earnings could grow significantly in this tax-sheltered account.

WHO CAN CONTRIBUTE

Any individual, even the designated beneficiary of the education IRA, may contribute. The designated beneficiary is the person on whose behalf the IRA has been established. Contributions on a child's behalf must end when the child reaches 18.

ELIGIBILITY

To make a full contribution to an education IRA, your modified adjusted gross income must be:
● $95,000 or less, if single;
● $150,000 or less, if married filing jointly.

You can make a partial contribution if your modified adjusted gross income is:
● Below $110,000 and you're single;
● Below $160,000 and you're married.

CONTRIBUTION LIMITS

The maximum contribution to an education IRA is $500 per year, per child, even if more than one person wants to contribute to the account.
What's deductible. You must pay taxes on earnings before you use the money to make contributions. Therefore, like Roth IRAS—but unlike traditional IRAs—contributions aren't deductible.

▼ PAY THE TAX CAT FIRST
You can contribute after-tax income to an education IRA. The money grows tax-free. The beneficiary can then withdraw the money according to the rules given above.

WHAT'S "QUALIFIED?"

There are seven types of qualified higher education expenses: tuition, fees, books, supplies, equipment, amounts contributed to a qualified state tuition program, and room and board. To be qualified, a higher education expense must also be:

- Incurred at an eligible educational institution, which is any college, university, vocational school, or other postsecondary educational institution. The institution must be eligible to participate in student aid programs administered by the Department of Education;
- Required for the enrollment or attendance of the designated beneficiary at the eligible education institution. Assuming any funds are left after the beneficiary is educated, they must be withdrawn within 30 days after that person reaches 30. The designated beneficiary may be changed to certain members of his or her family without any income tax being paid, if the new beneficiary is under age 30.

 16 An education IRA may affect the beneficiary's financial aid package.

WITHDRAWALS AND TAXES

The beneficiary can withdraw money at any time. Withdrawals are tax-free as long as they're no larger than the total of all qualified higher education expenses for at least a half-time student.

Earnings that have accumulated in the account are taxed when they're withdrawn. The formula can be complicated. Consult a tax advisor.

AGE LIMIT

All of the assets must be withdrawn by the time the designated beneficiary reaches age 30, or at the time the beneficiary dies (if younger than 30).

DEATH AND TAXES

T here's an old saying that says the only thing certain in life is death and taxes. That saying is particularly accurate when applied to IRAs. If you successfully build a large IRA, you face two potentially huge tax bills.

IRAs AND ESTATE TAXES

If you die and have a large IRA, your heirs may wind up paying taxes that could make you turn over in your grave.

For example, in the year 2000, estates worth more than $675,000 may ·be subject to federal estate taxes. Depending upon where you live, there may also be inheritance taxes. Both the traditional and Roth IRAs are included in the estate of the person who owned them. Therefore, the balance of all your IRA accounts at the time of your death is added to the value of your other property to determine whether or not estate taxes are owed—and if so, how much.

Normally, assets that go to your spouse, including IRAs, are not subject to estate taxes. That's why it's usually wise to name your spouse as the beneficiary of your estate.

Second-to-die rules. Your surviving spouse could have a very large estate that may be subject to considerable estate taxes upon his/her death. Unless your estate is small, therefore, it pays to consult an attorney who specializes in estate planning. Here are some rules you should know:

- Your IRA goes automatically to the beneficiary or beneficiaries you've named. It doesn't matter if you have a will or not. Like life insurance, it goes directly to the beneficiaries without going through the *probate* process. Probate is the act of distributing the assets under court supervision under the state's laws;

- Because IRAs enable middle-income people to accumulate significant wealth, many of them will face estate tax problems. If most of your estate consists of IRAs, and estate taxes are owed, it may not be liquid enough to pay the legal, administrative, and funeral expenses that come with dying. The death of an IRA owner can also cause income tax problems for the beneficiary.

17 With the Roth IRA, neither you nor your beneficiaries pay income taxes on the amounts that are withdrawn.

IRAs and Income Taxes

Along with the estate tax issues, dying may result in income tax problems for those left behind. Fortunately, beneficiaries won't pay the 10% penalty on IRA withdrawals from an inherited IRA, even if they're younger than 59 1/2. Here are some general rules.

Surviving spouses. A surviving spouse can avoid income taxes on an inherited IRA by directly rolling over the IRA into a Rollover IRA in his or her own name. No other beneficiary can take advantage of using this technique.

Estates. If your estate is named as the beneficiary rather than your spouse or another person, your estate may forfeit the ability to stretch out the distribution. If the beneficiary is someone other than your spouse, there are normally two choices. S/he may decide to either withdraw:

- The entire balance of the IRA by December 31 of the fifth year after the owner's death;
- A minimum amount each year based upon his or her life expectancy.

As mentioned earlier, traditional IRAs require you to begin withdrawals after age 70 1/2, whether you need the money or not. If the IRA owner began making mandatory minimum withdrawals prior to death, the beneficiary must continue making withdrawals at the same pace or faster.

Estimated Payments

Federal income tax withholding is required for distributions from IRAs unless you *elect out* of withholding on the distribution. However, if you elect out of withholding, you may have to make estimated tax payments. For more information on estimated tax payments see IRS Publication 505, Tax Withholding and Estimated Tax. You can view it at the IRS website at www.irs.gov.

401(κ)s

The 401(k) may be the best way to save taxes
and put away money for your future. This chapter
gives you an overview of the key points
that make a 401(k) so special.

WHAT'S A 401(κ)?

A 401(k) is an employer-sponsored savings program that enables you to set aside money for retirement.

A "BOX", NOT AN INVESTMENT

While many people think a 401(k) is an investment, it isn't. It's a plan created specifically for retirement investing. You contribute some of your salary to your account within the plan, and in that "box," you invest money according to your own personal goals and strategies.

FREE MONEY ▼
The money your employer contributes to your 401(k) plan is often referred to as "free money."

18 To have a 401(k) you must be employed at a company that sponsors one.

OVERRIDING RULES: THE GOVERNMENT

Two federal agencies supervise a set of rules and regulations that apply to all 401(k) plans.

The IRS. A 401(k) plan is a *tax-qualified* plan, which means both you and your company receive certain tax breaks if you each follow the IRS rules that qualify the plan for those breaks.

Department of Labor (DOL). This agency protects your rights as a plan participant, seeing that your employer and plan trustees comply with their required duties.

PLAN RULES: YOUR EMPLOYER

Your employer is the plan sponsor, the one who creates and runs the plan.

It's the job of your company's executives and benefits department to select the specific features of the plan, such as its investment options and contribution amounts that form a plan that falls within the federal rules and guidelines. Of course, no company-wide plan can be all things to all people. Decisions, therefore, must typically be based on the principle of creating the greatest good for the greatest number of people.

SELF-DIRECTED ACCOUNTS: YOU

At the plan's core is an investment account that you control.

Within limits set by the federal government and by the plan itself, the money you invest in your account qualifies for special tax protections.

The government created 401(k)s as an incentive for long-term savings. Your company created tools you may use that make sense for its specific plan. You, however, are the ultimate definer of your plan. You decide whether or not to participate, how much to contribute (within plan limits), what investments to buy, hold, and sell, when to withdraw money (within plan limits), and so on. Ultimately, your decisions determine how successful the 401(k) account will be toward achieving a comfortable retirement.

RULES WITHIN RULES

The Employee Retirement Income Security Act (ERISA) established rules that govern pensions and retirement plans. Company plans must comply with ERISA standards. Your plan may set different standards as long as it meets the minimum requirements established by ERISA.

THE COMPONENTS OF A 401(K)

E very plan must have certain functions in place in order to be in compliance with the federal rules for operating a 401(k) plan. Here are the services involved in running any 401(k) plan.

INVESTMENT MANAGEMENT

The heart of any 401(k) plan is how your investments are managed. Your employer is responsible for:

- Hiring one or more investment management firms to manage the money for all its employees;
- Selecting a diversified set of investments from which you may choose;
- Periodically reviewing the quality of the investments and the managers;
- Taking reasonable care in seeing that the employees' needs are met.

COMMUNICATIONS

This involves every aspect of helping participants learn about:

- The plan itself;
- How to use it;
- How investments are performing;
- How to make intelligent investment decisions.

Enrollment materials, brochures, fact sheets, disclosure documents, and your quarterly statement are just some of the informational products that fall within the category of plan communications.

ADMINISTRATION

This involves the procedural aspects of the plan, such as monitoring the plan, filing government-required documents, handling loans and other withdrawals, and adjusting procedures to meet all federal requirements. The administrator handles all of the paperwork that goes hand in hand with running a 401(k) plan smoothly.

RECORDKEEPING

In every 401(k) there's a legal responsibility to track all of the activity of every participant: what money goes in, what comes out, when contributions and company matching contributions are made, when investments are made, and so forth. The recordkeeper tracks all the activity on your account. Providing accurate and timely records is one of the most vital aspects of running a 401(k) plan. Without that, participants won't receive the proper information to make intelligent decisions at the proper times. It's the recordkeeper's job to send out quarterly statements.

SUMMARY PLAN DESCRIPTION

Take the time to thoroughly review all of the 401(k) materials supplied to you. The *Summary Plan Description* (SPD) lists the details of your plan and explains how it operates. An employer must provide you with an SPD, as well as an annual report.

TRUSTEE SERVICE

Your company has a *fiduciary* responsibility to see that the interests of all participating employees are protected. In fact, your company could be held accountable if something goes wrong with the plan. Therefore, one or more trustworthy people (trustees) are appointed to monitor the plan on behalf of the participants.

BUNDLED OR UNBUNDLED

Your employer must weigh the costs and benefits of one-stop shopping for all of the services (except trustee services) versus shopping individually for the best service in each category. Hiring one plan provider for all services may limit the plan to what the provider offers, but having all plan services handled seamlessly may mean faster, more efficient operations.

HOW A 401(K) PLAN WORKS

Ⓐll 401(k)s have a number of basic features in common. Some features' details may differ, though, based on the plan design. Here are some of the features you can find in 401(k) plans.

ELIGIBILITY

As a general rule, you must be at least 21 and have worked at least a year for the company in order to participate. Working more than 1,000 hours for the company during the year will normally be credited as a year of service, even if you weren't there for 12 full months. A company may offer more lenient eligibility rules, such as allowing contributions from your first day on the job.

HOW A CONTRIBUTION WORKS

When you elect to contribute money to a 401(k), you take a portion of your salary and postpone receiving it. Instead of it showing up in your paycheck, the money goes into your 401(k) account. Because it goes there before you receive it, the money isn't considered to be part of your taxable income.

Let's assume $100 goes into your 401(k). The full $100 is working for you. If you didn't put the money in a 401(k) and you're in the 28% tax bracket, you would only see $72 of it after taxes. Plus, if your employer makes a contribution on your behalf, that amount is also placed in the 401(k).

▼ YOU CAN'T TOUCH IT

A big difference between an individual retirement plan and a company retirement plan is that your paycheck must exclude your contribution. If the pay goes to you first, it can't be contributed tax-deferred. That's why you may see 401(k)s referred to with the unappealing—but accurate—label of salary reduction plan.

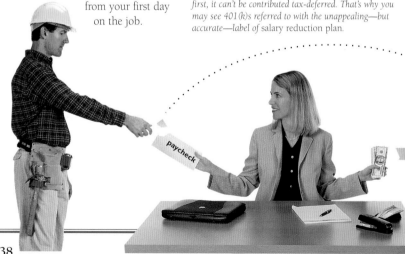

paycheck

AMOUNT YOU CAN PUT AWAY

When setting up the plan, your employer determines the maximum amount of money you're allowed to contribute on a pre-tax and after-tax basis. The amount you can contribute is a percentage of your salary. There is also a ceiling on the amount that's set by law.

EMPLOYER MATCH

In many plans, an employer contributes a certain amount of money for each dollar the employee contributes, up to a certain percentage of salary, usually 6%. An employee may not be entitled to keep this matching contribution until s/he has been employed for a specified length of time (see pgs. 40-41).

19 The maximum amount that an employee may contribute to a 401(k) on a pre-tax basis for the year 2000 is $10,500.

AFTER-TAX CONTRIBUTIONS

In many plans, you have the option to make additional contributions with *after-tax* money. This means that, in the year you make the contribution, you pay taxes on the amount contributed. Upon withdrawal, however, you pay no tax on that amount because you already paid it. Based on your situation, you may have to pay taxes on the money earned by the after-tax contributions. Consult a tax advisor regarding your specific situation.

TYPES OF INVESTMENTS

The best 401(k) plans offer choices to help you meet any investment objective. The best plans offer mutual funds from more than one company. You will have a wide variety of choices that include stocks, bonds, fixed income, and other investments.

WITHDRAWAL AND LOAN PROVISIONS

Most 401(k) plans permit you to borrow 50% of your *vested* (see pg. 40-41) balance up to a maximum of $50,000. You pay interest on the loan, even though it's your money, but the interest is credited to your own account.

KEEPING THE COMPANY MATCH

Vesting is an extremely important element of any plan that has a company matching contribution.

WHAT IT IS

Vesting refers to your rights to permanently own the money the employer contributes to your account. The time you have to wait to own that money depends on the vesting schedule rules of the plan. Once an amount has vested, you can take it with you if you leave the company. With some plans, the employer's contribution vests immediately. There are two other types of vesting schedules.

GRADED VESTING

With a *graded* vesting schedule, you gradually take ownership of the amount your employer has contributed. This plan is called graded because vesting is gradual until it's completed in a set number of years. Here's how a graded vesting schedule may look:

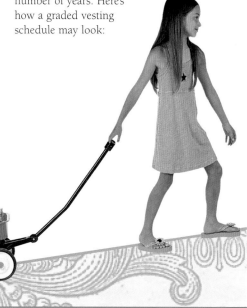

Number of years at that job	0-3	3	4	5	6	7
Percent vested	0	20	40	60	80	100

PLANNING FOR CHANGES

Whenever you're a participant in a 401(k) plan, make sure you understand the vesting schedule. If you're changing jobs and are close to vesting, consider staying until you vest. If you can't hold on until then, make sure the new offer compensates you for your loss. If you do lose money that wasn't vested, make sure you begin contributing to a 401(k) as soon as possible at your new place of employment and increase your contribution.

20 Vacation time generally counts toward the amount of time needed to become vested, unless you're paid in cash instead of time.

CLIFF VESTING

With *cliff* vesting, you're either fully vested or not vested at all. The employee takes full ownership of the employer's contribution after a certain number of years. If you end your employment before the specified number of years, your employer takes back all of its contribution.

An employer may adopt a vesting schedule that's no more restrictive than the schedule noted below. That means the employer may make it easier to vest, not harder. Shorter vesting periods make the plan more attractive to the company's workers and prospective employees.

Number of years at that job	Less than 7	At least 7
Percent vested	0	100

41

TAKING OUT MONEY

Sometimes borrowing from your 401(k) becomes necessary. Make sure you're borrowing for a legitimate purpose, not some impulsive purchase that you will regret later.

BORROWING

If your 401(k) has grown significantly, you may have a lot of money on paper, but very little in your pocket. Most company plans, however, permit you to borrow your own money from the plan. Here's how it works:

- You repay the loan and the interest charged on the loan is credited to your 401(k) account;
- Generally, the plan will limit loans to no more than half of the vested amount in your account up to a maximum of $50,000. There are other regulations that limit your loan, so you will need to check with your plan administrator. Typically, the loan must be repaid in full within five years;
- The plan may have other restrictions such as the size and number of loans. You may also be required to disclose your reasons for the loan.

21 You may need to consult a tax professional to be sure you won't be hit with a tax penalty.

THE DOWNSIDE OF BORROWING

At first glance, borrowing from a 401(k) may seem like an ideal solution, but there are several drawbacks:

- You may lose out on earning a better rate of return than the interest you're earning to repay the loan;
- You may lose some of the benefits of compound growth on the earnings removed from your account;
- If you leave your job, you're obligated to repay any loans against your retirement savings plan. Failing to repay the loan might be considered a distribution and you could be hit with a 10% premature withdrawal penalty.

 ◄ **IT LOOKS TEMPTING**
Your accumulated savings may seem enticing to borrow, but each day you keep your money from growing means less money you might have at the end.

THINGS TO KNOW

- Some 401(k) plans charge a fee for making loans. They do this to discourage loans and to recoup the cost of administering them.
- While most plans permit borrowing, consider using this feature only for extremely important expenses, such as a college education or a new house.

WITHDRAWING

Suppose you just want to close out your 401(k) and spend the money. You will pay a 10% penalty on the amount distributed, plus the taxes on that money. There are a number of situations that allow you to avoid the 10% penalty (but not the taxes) on the withdrawal. They include:

- You're at least 59 1/2;
- Death;
- Disability;
- Qualified Domestic Relations Order (QDRO);
- You're older than 55 and no longer a company employee;
- You're under 59 1/2, leave your job, and take substantially equal withdrawals based upon your life expectancy;
- You have medical expenses not covered by insurance that exceed 7.5% of your income.

22 No credit check is required with a 401(k) loan. If you don't repay the loan, you will simply have less in the account growing for you.

HARDSHIP WITHDRAWALS

The 401(k) plan will contain provisions to withdraw your money in the event of a financial emergency. The *hardship withdrawal* is the mechanism for taking money out in that situation. Unlike a loan, you don't have to repay a hardship withdrawal. Here are the conditions you need to meet in order to qualify for a hardship withdrawal:

- You must have an immediate and severe financial need;
- You can only take out the amount necessary to satisfy the financial need;
- You have to document the financial hardship and prove that other sources of funding are not available;
- You have to first use any other sources of funds which are available in your plan, such as loans.

Hardship withdrawals will hurt you financially. You may have to pay taxes on the amount withdrawn plus the 10% penalty. You may also be prohibited from making contributions again for a year.

LEAVING THE PLAN.

*I*t's becoming increasingly unlikely that you will spend your career with the same employer. A 401(k) is portable, which means you're free to take your money with you, minus any employer contributions that haven't vested. When leaving the company, you may have three options.

TAKE THE MONEY

You can take all or part of your money in cash. Your company will withhold 20% and send it to the IRS as a prepayment toward your income taxes. This protects the IRS from receiving nothing if you happen to spend everything you withdraw.

You may also pay a 10% *premature distribution* penalty, unless you meet one of the exceptions noted on pg. 43. You may also be liable to pay taxes on the amount you've taken out.

Most of all, you will probably miss out on earning a lot of money, because even small amounts can grow enormously over the years in a tax-deferred account (see pgs. 60-61).

LEAVE THE MONEY

Once you have at least $3,500 in your plan account, your company is required by federal law to offer you the option of keeping your money in the plan—even after you leave.

If your soon-to-be-former employer has better investment options than those available in your new plan, you may want to keep the money where it is and continue to invest it. You won't be allowed to add to your account, however.

Before making your decision, consider any administrative fees for non-employees or other rules that could affect you negatively.

If you leave your money, there will be no new tax consequences.

401(K)S AND DIVORCE

Divorce is a traumatic event in and of itself, but it can really traumatize a 401(k) plan. The plan may either be split or tapped as part of a property settlement. If so, the non-employee spouse's share must be taken pursuant to a Qualified Domestic Relations Order (QDRO) in order to avoid a 10% penalty on premature withdrawals. Any cash taken out of the 401(k) will be subject to income taxes unless the money is rolled over into an IRA. Consult a tax or other financial specialist and your benefits department for the rules governing QDROs.

TRANSFER THE MONEY

If you want to continue receiving the benefits of tax-deferred growth, consider transferring your money to another plan. If you take a new job with another company that offers its own 401(k), you may want to transfer your money into their plan. Check with your new employer's benefits department. Most, but not all, companies accept rollovers from an employee's previous place of work.

There are two ways to transfer money from your 401(k) account without triggering tax consequences.

Company-direct. Your employer will have a form for you to complete that authorizes the direct transfer of your money into your account in the new employer's plan. Since the money never technically leaves the shelter of a retirement plan, you avoid the 20% withholding and the 10% premature withdrawal penalty.

The indirect route. You can take the money as cash (minus the 20% withholding). You avoid any other tax consequences if you transfer it into a rollover IRA or another tax-qualified plan within 60 days. (Note: You will only have 80% of your total withdrawal. To roll over the entire amount and avoid a tax consequence, you will have to come up with the other 20% out of your own pocket. Any amount not transferred becomes subject to the 10% penalty and possibly income taxes.)

STAYING INFORMED

You will receive a lot of information from your employer regarding the ongoing status of your account and the overall company 401(k) plan. Keeping informed about how the plan works, what's happening in your specific account, and opportunities for investments are key to a successful plan.

BASIC INVESTMENT INFORMATION

Plans typically provide at least the following basic tools to help you understand your investment options.

Brochures. The plan provider (the company providing your plan) will usually give your employer brochures that explain the plan, and in particular, some basic guidelines for smart investing. Other brochures will try to explain how the plan works.

Fact sheets. You may receive sheets that detail the investment options you have, what you would be investing in, how each one has performed, and other vital data.

Magazines, newsletters. You may receive in-depth advice or general interest stories.

YOUR ACCOUNT'S STATUS

To keep current with the activity and value of your account, you may have a variety of resources at your disposal.

Account statement. At least once a year—typically once a quarter—you should receive a statement telling you where your money is invested, how much you and your employer have contributed, the status of any loans, and details of all activities since the last statement.

Toll-free phones. Many plans offer toll-free access to your account using your Personal Identification Number (PIN). Features typically include the ability to transfer money, change elections, and direct a host of other activities.

Online sites. Over time, access to your account through the Internet will become a common, even preferred, way of keeping tabs on, and managing, your account.

23 Read all notices sent by your employer. They may contain information which significantly changes how your plan works.

PLAN DETAILS

Upon enrollment, your employer should give you a booklet called the Summary Plan Description (SPD). Be aware, though, that it may have a more user-friendly title. This important reference document is your user's manual for the 401(k) plan. Although an SPD can appear lengthy, it is typically written from an objective perspective and is usually written in *plain English* (as opposed to legal language).

The purpose of an SPD is to give you quick access to every key element of your plan without all the legal language and minute details. Among its other features, an SPD also explains how to take action if you feel your rights have been violated. Expect to receive a new SPD every five years or so; sooner if there's been a major plan change.

The SPD is actually a summary of the Plan Document, which contains the full details in legal language. You may request a copy of the SPD or Plan Document from your employer's benefits department.

IN-DEPTH INVESTMENT ASSISTANCE

There are a wide variety of interactive tools for helping people customize answers to their own financial needs. Many employers also provide printed worksheets that serve the same function.

CHANGES IN THE PLAN

You may receive many legally required notices, particularly when there are substantive changes to your plan, such as adding or deleting investment options, altering loan rules, and so forth. Notices may come in newsletters, statement stuffers, or other materials.

24 Be aware that much of the information you receive has most likely been written by a marketing department and may contain biased information.

401(K) MISCELLANEOUS

Here are some other bits of information you might want to understand about 401(k)s.

A 401(K) OR AN IRA?

In an ideal world, you would have enough money to contribute to a 401(k) and an IRA. But if your financial situation is less than ideal, which should you choose?

Normally, a 401(k) is the better option. Generally, a worker will be able to put away more than the maximum amount allowed in an IRA. Your taxable income is reduced by the amount contributed to the 401(k).

Most of all, most 401(k)s offer an employer matching contribution.

24 After-tax contributions to a 401(k) can't be rolled over, but the earnings from those contributions can be rolled over.

OTHER IMPORTANT FACTS

Why companies offer 401(k) plans. A 401(k) plan is a part of every good employee benefits package. Like other benefits for employees, a 401(k) helps attract and keep good workers. Because employees are far less likely to work for the same company for their entire career, 401(k)s are extremely attractive. Workers can take the 401(k) with them when they leave the company.

Beware the limits. Your after-tax contributions to a qualified retirement plan must not bring your total contributions for the year beyond $30,000 contributed, or 25% of compensation, whichever is less.

If you leave and still have a loan. Many plans have a rule that require you to fully repay any oustanding loans from your account if your employment ends. Any portion you don't repay will be taxable. If you're under age 55, the money will also be subject to a 10% penalty tax.

Frozen savings. An employer is permitted to write the rules of a 401(k) plan so that distributions to all former employees aren't permitted until age 65. In addition, a plan isn't required to offer a loan feature. Be sure you understand the rules of your plan before you move to another employer.

IT'S A FACT

Unlike pensions, 401(k) plans are not insured by the Pension Benefit Guaranty Corporation, an agency of the federal government. They are insured by ?

IT'S A FACT

There is no longer a 15% excess distribution penalty. It was imposed on distributions exceeding $165,000 (and thefore penalized successful investors), but was repealed in 1997.

DEFINED BENEFIT PLANS VERSUS DEFINED CONTRIBUTION PLANS

A 401 (k) plan is considered a defined contribution plan. It differs from the traditional defined benefit plan. The old word for retirement planning used to be "pension." If you stayed with a company long enough, you'd receive a specified amount per month for life. Today there are two types of retirement programs. **Defined contribution plans.** With a defined contribution plan, specific amounts are contributed by the employee. Although the employer may match a percentage of the employee's contribution, the plan does not stipulate how much the employee will receive as a retirement benefit. That depends on the success of the investments and how the employee manages the account.

Defined benefit plans. The traditional pension falls under the heading of a defined benefit plan. In a defined benefit plan, the amount of benefits to be provided to each participant is spelled out clearly. The plan administrator calculates how much is needed to provide those benefits and the employer funds the required amount. Defined benefit plans are declining in popularity because of their expense, complexity, and the burden it places on the employer. The alternative is a defined contribution plan.

**THE FEATHER IN ▶
YOUR CAP**
Consider your 401(k) money as a feather in your cap. It's waiting for you to retire, to enjoy its benefits.

OTHER TYPES OF PLANS

There are a number of other retirement plans that resemble 401(k)s. All were designed to help you put away money for retirement in a tax-sheltered account.

SIMPLE IRAs

A SIMPLE IRA (Savings Incentive Match Plan for Employees) is a plan that allows employers and employees to have many of the benefits of a 401(k) without the administrative costs and complexities.

WHO'S ELIGIBLE?

SIMPLE IRAs are designed for the self-employed or an employee of a company with 100 employees or less. Normally, eligible employees must have received compensation in the previous calendar year of $5,000 or more. The employer may not maintain another qualified plan for employees. Like 401(k)s, SIMPLE IRAs reduce the participant's salary and the money is put away before income taxes are deducted.

HOW IT WORKS

Your employer contributes part of your salary to a retirement account set up on your behalf. As with many other retirement savings accounts, the salary you don't directly receive isn't taxed in that year, so your tax bill is reduced.

A SIMPLE IRA must comply with all the same IRA requirements and rules as any other IRA.

CONTRIBUTION LIMITS

The maximum employee contribution is $6,000 per year. Much like a 401(k), the contribution reduces the employee's salary, so less taxes are owed. The employer has two options with regard to its contributions:

- **Matching.** Employers must match the employee's elective contributions dollar-for-dollar up to 3% of the employee's compensation. The limit on the employer's contribution is $6,000. There is also a limit on how little the employer may contribute. It may not contribute less than 1% for any two years within a rolling five-year period;

- **Nonelective.** The second option is that the employer must make a contribution to a SIMPLE IRA on behalf of each employee who is eligible to participate. It doesn't matter if the employees make contributions on their own behalf. Contributions must be 2% of the employee's compensation, but reach a maximum employer contribution when the employee's salary reaches $160,000;

With either option, employees are vested immediately for all of the employer's contribution.

26 Keep October 1 in mind if you're planning to open a SIMPLE IRA. The plan must be established by October 1 of the year for which you're making a contribution. You have until the filing deadline to actually make the contribution.

RULES AND REGS

With the SIMPLE IRA, earnings grow in a tax-deferred account and are taxed upon withdrawal. The participant must begin withdrawals by age 70 1/2. You can still contribute to a Roth IRA, even if you have a SIMPLE IRA. Generally, the same withdrawal rules that apply to traditional IRAs are also applicable to SIMPLE IRAs. But here's one key difference. The penalty is 25% on the amount withdrawn, if you're younger than 59 1/2 and have been in the plan for less than two years. Otherwise, it's the typical 10% penalty on the amount withdrawn.

403(B) PLANS

W*hile most workers in the private sector have 401(k) plans, they're not the only type of employer-sponsored plan. A 403(b) plan takes its name from the Internal Revenue Code section that describes it.*

WHAT IT IS

A 403(b) plan is much like a 401(k) plan, except that it is designed for employees of public education institutions such as churches, schools and universities, museums, nonprofit hospitals, and charities.

403(b)s are often referred to as tax-sheltered annuity plans. Like 401(k)s, they allow employees to divert some of their salary, before taxes, into an account that grows on a tax-deferred basis until it's withdrawn.

ANNUITIES

According to the Financial Planning Association, the most controversial aspect of 403(b) plans is their annuity investment options, which usually have higher fees than no-load mutual funds. You also pay for the insurance component within the annuity and face a surrender charge if you switch to another investment within a specified number of years.

HOW IT WORKS

You can contribute as much as 20% of your annual income to a 403(b) plan. The maximum employee contribution for the year 2000 is $10,500.

You're less likely to have your contribution matched by an employer in a 403(b) plan than you are in a 401(k). When a match is offered, it usually vests immediately. Another unique feature of 403(b) plans is that you may have the opportunity to go beyond the normal contribution limits to make up for previous years in which you were below the maximum. If you retire before age 59 1/2, you can begin distributions without penalty if your plan allows it and you're at least 55.

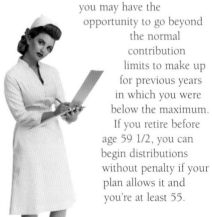

457 PLANS

Employees in the public sector have the opportunity to use a section 457 deferred compensation plan. They're available to most state and local government employees and are used to put away money to provide supplemental retirement income.

WHAT IT IS

You defer compensation on a pretax basis using a payroll deduction. 457 plans let you defer federal and usually state income taxes until your assets are withdrawn.

HOW IT WORKS

You can contribute up to one-third of your salary, up to a maximum of $8,000. That amount would be reduced by contributions to a 401(k) or 403(b) plan.

457 plans contain many of the same features found in 401(k) retirement savings plans which are used in the private sector.

IT'S A FACT

The name for this type of plan has the same, unexciting genesis as the 401(k) plan. A 457 plan is named after IRS Code 457.

THINGS TO KNOW

- You can't roll over money into an IRA, 401(k), or 403(b) plan from a 457 plan.

- The method and timing you choose for distributions from a 457 plan are irrevocable unless the plan permits changes. Even so, the plan must be written carefully to avoid unrestricted changes.

- The plan may permit you to defer the distribution date but not accelerate it.

27 Other tax-exempt organizations can have 457 plans, but only for highly compensated and management employees.

SEP IRAs

A *Simplified Employee Pension (SEP) is a retirement plan that permits employers to make deductible contributions on behalf of participating employees. A SEP is considered to be a defined contribution plan.*

WHO'S ELIGIBLE?

SEP IRAs are designed for the self-employed or an employee of a company with a SEP plan. To qualify, an employee must meet these conditions:

- The employee is at least 21 years old;
- S/he has worked for the employer during at least three out of the past five years;
- S/he has received at least $400 from the employer during the tax year.

In some instances, an independent contractor may meet the definition of qualifying employee.

An employer isn't required to offer employees this plan, even if it's set up for the employer. But once employees are included in the plan, the employer must contribute the same percentage for all employees.

27 With the advent of the SIMPLE and SEP IRAs, the Keogh plan has become less popular. There is significantly more paperwork with a Keogh plan.

RULES AND REGS

Distributions and withdrawals from a SEP are subject to traditional IRA rules. In addition, if you participate in either a SEP or a SIMPLE IRA, you can still contribute $2,000 to a traditional or Roth IRA.

CONTRIBUTION LIMITS

Employer contributions are discretionary. They may be as high as 15% of the employee's compensation up to $25,500.

All of the contributions to a SEP IRA immediately become the property of the account owner. There is no vesting.

A contribution can be made up through the due date on your tax return, including any extensions that are granted. Taxpayers are automatically entitled to extensions if Form 4868 (extension request) is filed by the tax return deadline. Nevertheless, the SEP plan must have been established by the original due date on the return (typically April 15, unless there's a different fiscal year).

KEOGHS

Keogh plans are designed for small businesses. Contributions to a Keogh will lower your tax bill, while you're saving for retirement. Like traditional IRAs, your contributions and earnings are sheltered from taxes until you begin making withdrawals.

WHO'S ELIGIBLE?

There are two types of Keoghs. **Money Purchase Keogh.** With the Money Purchase Keogh, you must select a percentage of your net income that you will contribute year after year. You can't change the percentage. On one hand, this type of Keogh is very inflexible. On the other, it forces you to save for retirement. You have a higher ceiling on contributions with this plan. **Profit-Sharing Keogh.** With a Profit-Sharing Keogh, you have more flexibility. If you're having a bad year, you don't have to make any contribution. You can vary your contribution from year to year. You have a lower ceiling on contributions with the profit sharing Keogh plan.

CONTRIBUTION LIMITS

Contribution limits differ between the two plans. To determine your net earnings, you must subtract your Keogh contribution. Here's what you could save:

- Money Purchase Keoghs permit you to put away as much as 25% of your net earnings from self-employment up to a maximum of $30,000;
- Profit-Sharing Keoghs limit your contribution to 15% of your net earnings from self-employment. The maximum is $25,500.

A contribution can be made up through the due date on the return, including any extensions that are granted. Taxpayers are automatically entitled to extensions if Form 4868 is filed by the tax return deadline. For contributions to count for the previous year, however, the Keogh must have been established by December 31 of the tax year for which you're filing.

RULES AND REGS

Even with a one-person plan, you may have to file a form in the 5500 series. The precise form depends upon the amount of assets in the plan and the number of participants. The form must be filed if assets are greater than $100,000 or you have more than one employee. The penalty for late filing is up to $1,000 per day.

STOCK PLANS

*M*anagement experts agree. Employees are more motivated if they own a piece of the company. Employee Stock Ownership Plans (ESOPs) and stock option plans accomplish that purpose. Here's how they work.

29 Warning: Exercising stock options may throw you into a different tax bracket.

ESOPs

An ESOP is a type of profit-sharing arrangement. With these plans, the company contributes shares of its stock to your retirement account or permits you to buy them at a discount from the market price.

Usually, the plan permits employees to accumulate money through payroll deduction and use the funds to purchase company stock at a discount. Some companies offer a pension plan or 401(k) to go along with the ESOP.

If you worry about your company's long-term future, you should start thinking about shifting money out of your ESOP at age 55.

There's a federal law that allows you to shift 25% of your assets in the ESOP account once you reach age 55, to other investments. When you hit age 60, you're permitted to shift 50% of the assets in your account to other investments.

DISTRIBUTIONS: STOCK OR CASH?

An ESOP must give you the option to demand distribution in the form of stock, except in limited circumstances (ask your benefits department). Distributions of employer stock may be taxed at capital gains rates rather than ordinary income tax rates. Therefore, it may be better for you to receive stock instead of cash. Ask your tax advisor.

STOCK OPTION PLANS

Stock options aren't just for high-level executives. More companies are offering them as an incentive to attract and keep key employees. The employee is granted the right to buy company stock at a set price for a specified length of time.

As an example, an employee is granted stock options, which permit her to buy 1,000 shares at $20 per share for the next 10 years. The stock goes up to $30 within that timeframe, so she exercises the option and makes $10 per share or $10,000. If the stock goes down and never goes above $20 during the 10 years, the employee's stock options would be worthless.

There are two types of stock option plans:

- With a *nonqualified stock option plan*, your profit is taxed at your ordinary tax rate. You pay taxes on the profit, which represents the difference between the value of the stock when the option was granted and the value of the stock when it's sold;

- With an *incentive stock option plan*, you normally pay capital gains taxes on the profit, which is a lower tax rate.

30 Review the diversification possibilities in the Summary Plan Description. There may be alternative investments provided or you may be able to roll over a portion of the ESOP into an IRA.

 31 Don't forget about state income taxes when you cash in stock options. It's possible you may also owe Social Security taxes.

INVESTING IN COMPANY STOCK

If you're a loyal employee and think highly of your employer, you might be inclined to put most of your money in company stock. There are several reasons why this can be a particularly dangerous strategy:

- You need to have a diverse investment portfolio. Banking your future on your company's stock is a risky proposition. One stock does not make a diversified portfolio. While there are examples of employees who became millionaires by investing exclusively in their employer's stock, the risks at most companies may exceed the potential reward;

- It's not just risky from an investment perspective. You also depend upon that employer for a paycheck. If business sours, you may find yourself faced with stock that's going down in value as well as the possibility of losing your job.

INVESTMENT STRATEGIES

To paraphrase an old Chinese saying, the largest
retirement account begins with the first contribution.
Whether you have an investment strategy or not,
saving money is the first step.

START NOW!

*The early bird is the big winner when it comes to saving for
retirement. In fact, saving money, even a dollar or two, can pay
off down the road.*

MAKE IT A HABIT

You should start saving money as soon
as you begin earning money. If you can
develop good saving habits at an early
age, they will follow you throughout
your life. The 80:20 rule works well.
Live on 80% of your paycheck and save
the remaining 20%. If you can't save
20%, start with a smaller percentage and
increase it gradually.

Try to avoid having spending rise to
the level of your income. When you get
a raise, consider banking the extra
money, since you've already proven you
can live on the lower amount.

IRAS FOR KIDS

Get children in the habit of saving
money as early as possible. Give them
an incentive. If you want your offspring
to be millionaires, you can make
annual contributions on their behalf to
an IRA. The only requirement is that
they have earned income equal to or
greater than the IRA contribution. That
means you may be able to pay them for
work and then put it into an IRA.
Consult a tax advisor.

THE POWER OF TAX-DEFERRED COMPOUND GROWTH

The chart to the right is only hypothetical, but it illustrates the power of tax deferred compound growth—how money can grow when it isn't removed to pay for taxes.

The example assumes $1,200 contributed every year with an 8% return and compares investing in a tax-deferred (the dollars) account to investing in a taxable account (the pennies). Because every dollar in the tax-deferred account is reinvested, the end result can be dramatic.

COMPOUND GROWTH

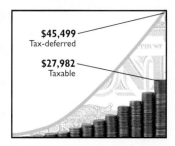

$45,499 Tax-deferred

$27,982 Taxable

OTHER EXAMPLES

Starting at 25. If you start saving at age 25 and invest $100 per month for 20 years, you will have more than $275,000 at age 65 if you assume an 8% annual rate of return. If you wait until age 40 and save $100 per month for 20 years, your tax-deferred account will be worth less than $90,000 at age 65.

Starting at 21. If you're age 21 and put away $2,000 per year from age 21 to 30, you will have thousands more at age 65 than someone who saves $2,000 per year from age 31 to 65. The $20,000 contributed from age 21 to 30 will grow into a much larger nest egg than the investor who contributed every year from age 31 to 65.

Starting at 19 1/2. If you put away $25 a week for 40 years and earn 7%, you will have more than $286,000 at retirement.

PREPARING TO INVEST

*I*t's time to sit down with your spouse or life partner, if you have one, and discuss where to invest that money you're putting away for the future. You need to decide upon a strategy for investing.

HOW RATES OF RETURN AFFECT GROWTH

Although it pays to start saving early for retirement, you also need to take some amount of risk to solidify your financial future. Financial planners are virtually unanimous in their opinion that equity (stock) investments are the right choice for long-term investors. Historically, the stock market has returned an average of approximately 12% per year.

Doubling your money. While conservative investors might shy away from the stock market, experts suggest using the *rule of 72, which* offers a clear demonstration of why it's important to seek a higher rate of return. To determine how long it takes for your money to double, you divide the number 72 by the rate of return. Here are some examples that show how the rule of 72 works:

● If you get a 6% return on your investment, it will take 12 years for your money to double, since 72 divided by 6 equals 12;

● If you achieve a 9% rate of return, your money will double in 8 years, since 72 divided by 9 equals 8;

● If you get a 12% rate of return, your money will double in 6 years, since 72 divided by 12 equals 6.

32 Historically, over any 10-year period, stocks have outperformed every other investment.

RECOVERY TIMES AFTER BEAR MARKETS

This chart shows the number of months it took each major bear market to recoup its losses. Time tends to reduce the risk of loss.

Bear Market Dates	S&P 500 Total Return	Months to Recoup
1/62 - 6/62	-22.3%	13
12/68 - 6/70	-29.3%	28
1/73 - 9/74	-42.6%	42
12/80 - 7/82	-16.9%	23
9/87 - 11/87	-29.5%	21

HOW MUCH TIME?

As you age, your risk tolerance generally becomes less. Most people realize their days in the work force are numbered and they won't be getting a paycheck for too much longer. When you need the money you've invested in the immediate future, you may become more concerned about fluctuations in value (volatility) than in growth. That's because an investment that's down in the dumps won't necessarily regain its value before you need to sell it.

Your tolerance for risk usually decreases as the time draws near when you need to cash in your investment. The time when you need to use the money is called your time horizon. If it's going to be twenty years until you need the money, you can take more chances than someone who needs the money a year or two from now.

HOW MUCH MONEY?

If you have money coming in from a number of sources, your tolerance for risk may be higher. That's because you could make an investment without feeling you're losing your life's savings. Individuals with fewer financial resources can't be as aggressive in their investing, because they're dealing with a large percentage of the money they will depend upon to live.

For example, if your 401(k) is the only investment you're banking on to fund your retirement, you may need to be more conservative than someone who has other resources to draw upon when the time comes to retire. Someone with real estate investments, savings accounts, IRAs, or other types of investments is in a much more secure position.

A WORD ABOUT RISK

Even when you pick the safest investment, your money is still at risk. You risk the possibility that inflation will eat away at the money you're earning on that investment. In effect, you would be losing money if your rate of return is less than the rate of inflation. As an example, bonds are commonly perceived as a great way to provide income. Although they pay income on a regular basis, if your return is less than the rate of inflation, you will actually be losing money invisibly. You're also at risk if you want to sell your bonds before the maturity date, because the value of the bonds will be lower if interest rates go up. The value of the bond fluctuates in relation to interest rates.

THREE MAIN STRATEGIES

B efore investing, you need to determine what you want your money to do for you. In investing, there are essentially three main ways, or strategies you can use to try to reach your goals.

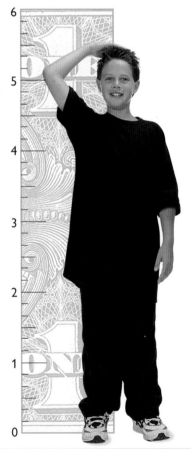

GROWTH

One main strategy is to grow your money—even, in some cases, as much money as you can. A growth strategy requires investors to give up the most control as well as a significant level of predictability concerning the success of the strategy.

In return for unpredictability and loss of control, growth investors expect to be more highly compensated than income or protection investors, and within a reasonable time period. If the compensation—in the form of a stock price increase, for example, doesn't materialize, the investors can sell and take back as much of their money as they can.

Growth investments typically come in two categories:

Stocks. This category has the greatest potential for growth.

Mutual funds. Growth mutual funds are usually considered less risky than stocks alone because they spread risk out over a number of different stocks. (For more information on how these investments should fit into your portfolio, see pgs. 64-65.)

INCOME

The second main strategy is to earn income. You can choose to earn relatively predictable amounts at a lower risk level than from growth investments.

This means earning an income that will not only outpace inflation, but provide some additional money. Investing to earn income is for people who want to receive regular installments of money, or want at least some predictability in the amount they can earn, or when they will earn it.

Investors with income as a main strategy allow others to use their money for longer periods of time than they would allow if they were protecting their money. In return, they expect to be better compensated for taking the added risk that's a by-product of having less control.

If your strategy is to earn income, you will typically buy bonds, bond funds, or invest in mutual funds whose primary objective is to earn income. (For example, a utility stock fund typically pays better dividends than other stock funds.)

33 You may read materials that describe these as goals, but in reality, they are the main strategies for reaching your goals.

PROTECTION

The third strategy is simply to hold onto what you've already saved. This means you will protect your money by investing it in relatively safe investments.

With investments, safety doesn't translate into a do-nothing approach. To the contrary, doing nothing with money or keeping it in a no-interest account allows inflation to erode its buying power until it has less value than when you started. For protection, therefore, investors try to keep close control over their money by lending it for short periods to borrowers who have proven, reliable reputations.

Since borrowers can't do much with money they have to repay quickly, they typically don't pay much interest. That's an acceptable trade-off for investors who consider an investment to be successful if it earns enough to offset inflation and protects their money until they need it.

Some of the investments you might consider to protect your money are money market funds, money market mutual funds, and other short-term "parking places."

(For more information on types of protection investments, see pgs. 64-65).

Asset Allocation

Financial experts recommend an investment strategy called asset allocation. To pursue this strategy, you divide your investments among different types of assets such as stock, bonds, and cash. There are several reasons why this strategy is recommended by many financial experts.

Why Allocate?

Each asset class coincides neatly with helping you achieve one of the three different strategies. Proponents of asset allocation also believe that investment success may depend most of all on what percentages you've allocated among the different asset classes. Other asset groups include real estate and hard assets like gold, but they're usually inappropriate for retirement plans because of their higher risks.

Stocks

Many companies are owned by people like you. A company divides its ownership into equal shares and sells them to the public. If you own its stock, you share in the success if it does well, and in the failure if it doesn't. In short, most people buy stock to let their fortunes ride with the fortunes of the company.

There are many types of stocks.

Speculative stocks. These are the start-up, or relatively new companies who have not yet established themselves in their product or service market. They may also be companies in high risk businesses, such as the Internet, biotechnology, and a number of other highly competitive and money-intensive industries.

Growth stocks. These are companies that have moved beyond the phase of uncertainty but still have a lot of room to grow. The more and faster they grow, the more stock price movement investors can expect to see.

Value stocks. These are well-established companies with histories of consistent earnings and growth.

Income stocks. These are companies that do not need to use their profits to grow. They share much of their profits with investors in the form of dividends.

YOUR NEST EGG▼

Depending upon what your nest looks like, you may need to put different eggs into it. Your strategy should determine the contents of your nest.

BONDS

When you buy fixed income securities, typically bonds, you're lending money to earn some income. There's no need to invest in tax-free bonds since retirement accounts provide tax protection anyway.

Buying bonds reflects a decision to make income a higher priority than protection. How much more of a priority is still a matter of degree you can control.

U.S. government bonds. These bonds are nearly risk-free and usually offer fairly low interest rates. This makes them attractive to very conservative investors.

Short-term fixed income funds. The fund manager lends your money for somewhat longer periods than s/he does in money market funds, but still with relatively low risk.

Corporate bonds. Corporations often finance major projects by issuing bonds rather than selling stock, primarily because of tax regulations. Corporate bonds and bond funds typically offer higher interest rates than their government counterparts since the interest is fully taxable and the risks may be somewhat higher (but not necessarily significantly higher).

The higher interest rates can make corporate bonds and bond funds more attractive to investors with tax-protected retirement accounts.

CASH EQUIVALENTS

Since one strategy is to protect what you've already saved, there are investments designed with safety as the top priority. By investing in securities from an asset class called *cash equivalents*, you try to protect your money and earn a little income at the same time.

They are securities that let you keep your money close and safe by lending it for very short periods (a day to a year) to borrowers with reliable reputations. Investments designed for protection are called cash equivalents because in practice, they're designed to be almost as safe as cash.

Money market funds. These are similar to savings accounts except your money is pooled with other customers into one large sum. The money is then loaned to businesses or government entities for a short time, usually a week or less and sometimes overnight.

Money market funds are considered one of the safest investments. The interest earned is shared by all the customers and the bank takes a small fee for its efforts. Bank money market funds are federally insured. Money market mutual funds usually have private insurance, which has been very safe but isn't as safe as federal insurance.

DOLLAR COST AVERAGING

Dollar cost averaging is a good investment strategy for a retirement plan. It disciplines you into saving money that you otherwise might spend.

WHO IS IT FOR?

This most basic of strategies is good for investors who are resistant to investing, or at least uncomfortable with using their money in a way that they don't fully understand. It's also good for people who can afford to invest only small amounts at a time. For many people, it's simply a way to overcome inertia and become an investor.

HOW IT WORKS

There are three parts to dollar cost averaging.

The investment. You select the type of investment to put your money into;

The timing. You select a regularly scheduled date that coincides with your paycheck (or another logical time);

The amount. You select the amount you feel you can afford to invest at each interval (for example, an amount you might otherwise spend on impulsive purchases you will soon forget).

As the example below shows, you could decide to invest $500 in a mutual fund on the first day of each month. Then you pick a date to make the first investment—and the process begins.

DAY ONE	DAY 31 (MONTH 2)	DAY 61 (MONTH 3)
The stock price is $5. You invest $500. That buys 100 shares.	The stock price is now $16.67. You invest $500. That buys 30 shares. Total shares: 130. Your average price per share = $7.69.	The stock price is $8. You invest $500. That buys 62 shares. Total shares: 192. Your average price per share = $7.81.

IT REMOVES THE GUESSWORK

Dollar cost averaging offers you choices. You can invest:

- In stocks, bonds, or mutual funds;
- On a regular schedule automatically;
- Any amount of money you want for each investment.

IT DOESN'T REQUIRE MUCH MONEY

The point is to accumulate a lot of shares over time without using a lot of money each time. Since you're not investing all at once, you don't need to have much money to begin. You may even be able to stick to the plan by transferring money directly from your checking account each month.

CONTRIBUTING TO YOUR RETIREMENT PLAN

By using dollar cost averaging, you will be making your contributions throughout the year. It pays for you to make your contributions as early in the year as possible, rather than waiting for the tax deadline. Your money will have more time to grow and you will amass much more over the years. If making your contribution in one large chunk isn't possible, you can arrange for the money to be deducted in installments from a checking or savings account.

IT'S METHODICAL

Once you begin, you stick with the plan—no matter what happens to the price. Sometimes your money buys more shares; other times, it buys fewer shares.

DAY 91 (MONTH 4)	DAY 121 (MONTH 5)
The stock price is up to $9. You invest $500. That buys 55 shares. Total shares: 247. Your average price per share = $8.10.	*The stock price is $6. You invest $500. That buys 83 shares. Total shares: 330. Your average price per share = $7.58.*

◀ AN EXAMPLE

As you can see here, the price of the investment changes, but your investment stays on a regular schedule, with the same amount invested each month. This is a disciplined, relatively painless strategy for contributing to any retirement plan that can add up to significant savings over time.

WHO CAN HELP?

Retirement savings plans represent a large amount of the assets that many of us will live on when we leave the work force. Because so much is at stake, you may need to turn to others to help with your retirement planning. Here are a few ways to help you find the right financial advisor and some tips for what you can do to help yourself.

FINANCIAL ADVISORS

Ask friends and business associates for the names of three or more trusted financial advisors.

Evaluate the advisor's credentials. A Certified Financial Planner (CFP) designation means the advisor has extensive training and abides by a strict ethical code. Some Certified Public Accountants (CPAs) also hold the Personal Financial Specialist (PFS) designation and provide advice on financial planning.

Ask how the financial advisor makes money. Some financial planners charge on an hourly or project basis. Others charge a percentage of the assets they manage for you. Some charge nothing but make a commission on the products they recommend. A number of financial planners charge a set fee for their advice, but also make money on the products they sell you. The financial advisor should be willing to fully disclose any and all fees. Make sure the advisor has roots in your community and is in business for the long-term.

Check history. Before dealing with any broker or financial professional, place a call to the National Association of Securities Dealers (NASD) at 800-289-9999 and check on the individual's disciplinary record. The NASD's website is www.nasd.com. You can also investigate a financial advisor by contacting the state agency that regulates securities.

WEBSITES

National Association of Securities Dealers Regulatory Division (NASD): www.nasdr.com;

The Financial Planning Association: www.fpanet.org

U.S. Department of Labor: www.dol.gov;

Internal Revenue Service: www.irs.gov;

Employee Benefit Research Institute: www.ebri.org;

Securities Exchange Commission: www.sec.gov.

YOUR EMPLOYER

Many employers are trying to help employees make wise retirement planning choices. A caring employer does more than just set up a retirement savings plan for employees. Many companies are now arranging for their employees to receive objective and impartial advice on what investments to choose in their employer-sponsored plan.

34 The best advisors are objective and concerned with your best interests, not in selling you a particular financial product.

YOURSELF

The most important person to rely on is you. You have the ultimate responsibility of saving and investing for retirement. By becoming knowledgeable about your finances and planning for retirement, you will make the right decisions for you and your family. You've taken the first step by reading this book.

IT'S A FACT

There are more than 200,000 401(k) plans with assets of more than $1 trillion. Over 25 million people participate in 401(k) plans.

THINGS TO KNOW

The Department of Labor can provide help if your employer refuses to give you information about your retirement plans. The phone number is 202-219-8776. You may also write to U.S. Department of Labor, 200 Constitution Avenue NW, Washington, DC, 20210.

INDEX

ACKNOWLEDGMENTS

AUTHORS' ACKNOWLEDGMENTS

The production of this book has called on the skills of many people. A special thanks to the sponsors and staff of the Employee Benefit Research Institute over the past 22 years, without whom this work would not be possible. We would also like to thank our editors at Dorling Kindersley, and our consultant, Nick Clemente. Marc wishes to dedicate this book to Zachary Robinson for his great patience and support when it was most needed. Special thanks to Teresa Clavasquin for her generous support and assistance.

PUBLISHER'S ACKNOWLEDGMENTS

Dorling Kindersley would like to thank everyone who worked on the Essential Finance series, and the following for their help and participation:

Editorial Stephanie Rubenstein; **Design and Layout** Jill Dupont; **Consultants** Nick Clemente; Skeeter; **Indexer** Rachel Rice; **Proofreader** Stephanie Rubenstein; **Photography** Anthony Nex; **Photographers' Assistants** Damon Dulas;**Models** Jane Cho, Sherry Lawrence, Sarah Lawrence, Frank Wolf, Kara Rubenstein, Stephanie Fowler, Willa Dorn Lilien, Zachary Robinson, Harold Rose, Joshua Tohl, Tom Dupont, Elizabeth Pepper, Bud Lieberman, Mimi Lieberman; **Picture Researcher** Mark Dennis; Sam Ruston

AUTHORS' BIOGRAPHIES

Dallas Salisbury is President and CEO of the Employee Benefit Research Institute (EBRI), in Washington, DC. EBRI was founded in 1978 to provide objective, unbiased information regarding the employee benefit system and related economic security issues. Dallas joined EBRI at its founding in 1978. Dallas is also chairman and CEO of the American Savings Education Council (ASEC), and the Consumer Health Education Council (CHEC). Both are partnerships of public and private-sector institutions that undertake initiatives to raise public awareness regarding what is needed to ensure long-term economic and health security. Dallas is a Fellow of the National Academy of Human Resources, the recipient of the 1997 Award for Professional Excellence from the Society for Human Resources Management and the 1998 Keystone Award of "WorldatWork." He has served on the Secretary of Labor's ERISA Advisory Council and the Presidential PBGC Advisory Committee. He currently serves as a member of the Advisory Committee to the Comptroller to the United States, the 2001 Board of Directors for the Society of Human Resource Management, and on the GAO Advisory Group on Social Security and Retirement. Prior to joining EBRI, Dallas held full-time positions with the Washington State Legislature, the U.S. Department of Justice, the Pension Benefit Guaranty Corporation (PBGC), and the Pension and Welfare Benefits Administration of the U.S. Department of Labor. He holds a B.A. degree in finance from the University of Washington and an M.A. in public policy and administration from the Maxwell School at Syracuse University.

Marc Robinson is co-founder of Internet-based moneytours.com, a personal finance resource for corporations, universities, credit unions, and other institutions interested in helping their constituents make intelligent decisions about their financial lives. He wrote the original *The Wall Street Journal Guide to Understanding Money and Markets*, created *The Wall Street Journal Guide to Understanding Personal Finance*, co-published a personal finance series with Time Life Books, and wrote a children's book about onomateopia in different languages. In his two decades in the financial services industry, Marc has provided marketing consulting to many top Wall Street firms. He is admitted to practice law in New York State.